50 Premium Keto Recipes for Dinner

By: Kelly Johnson

Table of Contents

- Zucchini Noodles with Pesto and Grilled Chicken
- Garlic Butter Shrimp with Asparagus
- Keto Meatloaf with Creamy Mashed Cauliflower
- Baked Salmon with Lemon Dill Sauce
- Beef Stroganoff with Shirataki Noodles
- Cauliflower Fried Rice with Chicken
- Keto Chicken Parmesan
- Eggplant Lasagna
- Pork Belly with Roasted Brussels Sprouts
- Keto Fish Tacos with Avocado Salsa
- Chicken Thighs with Garlic Mushroom Sauce
- Cheesy Broccoli and Cauliflower Casserole
- Keto Steak with Herb Butter
- Grilled Lamb Chops with Mint Yogurt Sauce
- Shrimp and Sausage Skillet
- Keto Stuffed Bell Peppers
- Spinach and Feta Stuffed Chicken Breast
- Eggplant and Ground Beef Moussaka
- Lemon Herb Grilled Chicken with Zucchini
- Keto Chili with Ground Beef
- Pork Chops with Avocado Cream Sauce
- Baked Chicken with Parmesan Crust
- Keto Meatballs in Tomato Sauce
- Crispy Parmesan Crusted Salmon
- Keto BBQ Ribs
- Zucchini and Tomato Gratin
- Keto Beef Tacos in Lettuce Wraps
- Salmon and Avocado Salad
- Keto Chicken and Vegetable Stir-Fry
- Garlic Butter Steak Bites
- Cauliflower Mac and Cheese
- Keto Beef Wellington
- Keto Shrimp Scampi
- Crab Cakes with Lemon Aioli
- Keto Broccoli Cheese Soup

- Grilled Chicken with Avocado Salsa
- Keto Pork Stir Fry
- Creamy Tuscan Chicken
- Keto Mushroom and Swiss Burger
- Eggplant Parmesan
- Keto Cabbage Stir Fry
- Keto Stuffed Mushrooms
- Chicken Alfredo with Zucchini Noodles
- Keto Chicken Piccata
- Beef and Broccoli Stir Fry
- Crispy Skin Duck Breast with Cauliflower Puree
- Keto Shrimp and Avocado Salad
- Keto Cheeseburger Salad
- Grilled Pork Tenderloin with Garlic Butter
- Keto Shrimp and Spinach Casserole

Zucchini Noodles with Pesto and Grilled Chicken

Ingredients:

For the Zucchini Noodles:

- 2 medium zucchini (spiralized into noodles, or use a julienne peeler)
- 1 tablespoon olive oil
- Salt and pepper, to taste

For the Grilled Chicken:

- 2 boneless, skinless chicken breasts
- 1 tablespoon olive oil
- Salt and pepper, to taste
- 1 teaspoon garlic powder (optional)
- 1 teaspoon paprika (optional)

For the Pesto:

- 1 cup fresh basil leaves
- 1/4 cup pine nuts (or walnuts, if preferred)
- 2 cloves garlic, minced
- 1/2 cup extra virgin olive oil
- 1/4 cup grated Parmesan cheese
- Salt and pepper, to taste
- 1 tablespoon lemon juice (optional, for a fresh kick)

Instructions:

1. **Prepare the Grilled Chicken**:
   Preheat your grill or grill pan over medium-high heat.
   Rub the chicken breasts with olive oil, salt, pepper, garlic powder, and paprika.
   Grill the chicken for about 6-7 minutes on each side (depending on thickness) until fully cooked and the internal temperature reaches 165°F (75°C).
   Let the chicken rest for a few minutes, then slice it into thin strips.
2. **Make the Pesto**:
   In a food processor or blender, combine the basil, pine nuts, garlic, Parmesan cheese, salt, and pepper.
   With the processor running, slowly drizzle in the olive oil until everything is

smooth and emulsified.

Add lemon juice if using, and adjust seasoning to taste.

3. **Prepare the Zucchini Noodles**:

    Heat a large skillet over medium heat and add the olive oil.

    Add the zucchini noodles to the pan, season with salt and pepper, and sauté for 2-3 minutes. You want the zucchini to soften slightly but still have some crunch, so avoid overcooking.

    If you'd like to remove excess moisture, you can briefly pat the zucchini noodles with a paper towel.

4. **Assemble the Dish**:

    In a large bowl, toss the zucchini noodles with the pesto until evenly coated.

    Plate the pesto zucchini noodles and top with the sliced grilled chicken.

5. **Serve**:

    Garnish with additional Parmesan cheese and fresh basil leaves, if desired.

    Serve immediately and enjoy!

Garlic Butter Shrimp with Asparagus

Ingredients:

- 1 lb large shrimp, peeled and deveined
- 1 bunch asparagus, trimmed and cut into 2-inch pieces
- 3 tablespoons butter
- 4 cloves garlic, minced
- 1 tablespoon olive oil
- 1 teaspoon lemon juice
- Salt and pepper, to taste
- Fresh parsley, chopped (for garnish)

Instructions:

1. **Cook the Asparagus**: Heat 1 tablespoon of olive oil in a large skillet over medium heat. Add the asparagus and sauté for 3-4 minutes until tender. Remove from the skillet and set aside.
2. **Cook the Shrimp**: In the same skillet, melt the butter over medium heat. Add the garlic and cook for 1-2 minutes until fragrant. Add the shrimp, salt, pepper, and cook for 2-3 minutes on each side until pink and cooked through.
3. **Combine**: Add the cooked asparagus back into the skillet and toss with the shrimp and garlic butter. Stir in the lemon juice and adjust seasoning to taste.
4. **Serve**: Garnish with fresh parsley and serve immediately.

Keto Meatloaf with Creamy Mashed Cauliflower

For the Meatloaf:

- 1 lb ground beef (or a mix of beef and pork)
- 1/4 cup almond flour
- 1/4 cup grated Parmesan cheese
- 1 egg
- 2 tablespoons heavy cream
- 2 cloves garlic, minced
- 1 teaspoon dried oregano
- 1 teaspoon dried basil
- Salt and pepper, to taste
- 1/4 cup sugar-free ketchup (for topping)

For the Mashed Cauliflower:

- 1 medium head cauliflower, cut into florets
- 1/4 cup heavy cream
- 2 tablespoons butter
- Salt and pepper, to taste
- 1/4 cup grated Parmesan cheese

Instructions:

1. **Make the Meatloaf**:
   Preheat the oven to 375°F (190°C). In a large bowl, combine the ground beef, almond flour, Parmesan cheese, egg, heavy cream, garlic, oregano, basil, salt, and pepper. Mix until well combined.
   Shape the mixture into a loaf and place it in a baking dish. Top with the sugar-free ketchup and bake for 35-40 minutes, or until cooked through.
2. **Make the Mashed Cauliflower**:
   Steam the cauliflower florets until tender (about 10-12 minutes). Once tender, transfer to a food processor or blender with the heavy cream, butter, salt, and pepper. Blend until smooth. Stir in Parmesan cheese for extra flavor.
3. **Serve**:
   Slice the meatloaf and serve alongside the creamy mashed cauliflower. Enjoy this comforting keto meal!

Baked Salmon with Lemon Dill Sauce

Ingredients:

- 4 salmon fillets (skin-on or skinless)
- 2 tablespoons olive oil
- Salt and pepper, to taste
- 1 tablespoon lemon zest
- 1 tablespoon fresh lemon juice
- 1/4 cup sour cream
- 2 tablespoons mayonnaise
- 1 tablespoon fresh dill, chopped
- 1 teaspoon Dijon mustard

Instructions:

1. **Prepare the Salmon**:
   Preheat the oven to 400°F (200°C). Place the salmon fillets on a baking sheet lined with parchment paper. Drizzle with olive oil and season with salt, pepper, and lemon zest.
2. **Bake the Salmon**:
   Bake for 12-15 minutes, or until the salmon easily flakes with a fork and is cooked to your desired doneness.
3. **Make the Lemon Dill Sauce**:
   In a small bowl, combine the lemon juice, sour cream, mayonnaise, dill, and Dijon mustard. Mix until smooth.
4. **Serve**:
   Serve the baked salmon with a generous dollop of the lemon dill sauce on top. Garnish with extra fresh dill, if desired.

Beef Stroganoff with Shirataki Noodles

Ingredients:

- 1 lb beef sirloin or tenderloin, sliced into thin strips
- 2 tablespoons olive oil
- 1/2 onion, finely chopped
- 3 cloves garlic, minced
- 1 cup mushrooms, sliced
- 1 cup beef broth (low-sodium)
- 1/2 cup heavy cream
- 2 tablespoons Dijon mustard
- Salt and pepper, to taste
- 2 packs Shirataki noodles (or zucchini noodles as an alternative)
- Fresh parsley, chopped (for garnish)

Instructions:

1. **Cook the Beef**: Heat olive oil in a large skillet over medium-high heat. Add the beef and cook until browned, about 3-4 minutes. Remove from the skillet and set aside.
2. **Cook the Vegetables**: In the same skillet, add onion, garlic, and mushrooms. Sauté until soft, about 5 minutes.
3. **Make the Sauce**: Add the beef broth, Dijon mustard, and heavy cream. Stir to combine and bring to a simmer. Cook for 3-4 minutes until the sauce thickens.
4. **Combine and Serve**: Add the beef back to the skillet, stirring to coat with the sauce. Season with salt and pepper. In a separate pan, quickly sauté the Shirataki noodles according to package instructions, then add them to the skillet. Toss to combine. Garnish with fresh parsley and serve!

Cauliflower Fried Rice with Chicken

Ingredients:

- 2 cups cauliflower rice (fresh or frozen)
- 1 lb chicken breast, diced
- 2 tablespoons olive oil
- 1/2 onion, chopped
- 1 cup mixed vegetables (carrots, peas, and bell pepper)
- 2 cloves garlic, minced
- 2 eggs, lightly beaten
- 3 tablespoons soy sauce or coconut aminos
- Salt and pepper, to taste
- Green onions, chopped (for garnish)

Instructions:

1. **Cook the Chicken**: Heat olive oil in a large skillet over medium-high heat. Add the chicken and cook until browned and cooked through, about 6-7 minutes. Remove from the skillet and set aside.
2. **Prepare the Fried Rice**: In the same skillet, add the onion, garlic, and mixed vegetables. Sauté until softened, about 5 minutes.
3. **Add the Cauliflower Rice**: Stir in the cauliflower rice and cook for 5-7 minutes, until slightly tender.
4. **Scramble the Eggs**: Push the cauliflower rice to one side of the skillet, and pour the beaten eggs into the other side. Scramble until fully cooked.
5. **Combine**: Add the cooked chicken back to the pan, along with soy sauce or coconut aminos. Stir to combine and cook for 2 more minutes.
6. **Serve**: Garnish with chopped green onions and serve!

Keto Chicken Parmesan

Ingredients:

- 4 boneless, skinless chicken breasts
- 1 cup almond flour
- 1/2 cup grated Parmesan cheese
- 2 eggs, beaten
- 1 cup marinara sauce (sugar-free)
- 1 1/2 cups shredded mozzarella cheese
- 2 tablespoons olive oil
- Salt and pepper, to taste
- Fresh basil, chopped (for garnish)

Instructions:

1. **Preheat the Oven**: Preheat the oven to 400°F (200°C). Place a rack in the middle.
2. **Bread the Chicken**: In a shallow bowl, combine almond flour, Parmesan cheese, salt, and pepper. Dip each chicken breast in the beaten eggs, then coat with the almond flour mixture.
3. **Cook the Chicken**: Heat olive oil in a skillet over medium-high heat. Cook the chicken breasts for 3-4 minutes per side, until golden brown.
4. **Bake**: Place the browned chicken breasts on a baking sheet. Top each with marinara sauce and mozzarella cheese. Bake for 10-12 minutes, or until the cheese is melted and bubbly.
5. **Serve**: Garnish with fresh basil and serve with a side of roasted veggies or zucchini noodles.

Eggplant Lasagna

Ingredients:

- 2 large eggplants, sliced into thin rounds
- 1 lb ground beef or turkey
- 1/2 onion, chopped
- 2 cloves garlic, minced
- 2 cups marinara sauce (sugar-free)
- 2 cups ricotta cheese
- 1 egg
- 2 cups shredded mozzarella cheese
- 1/2 cup grated Parmesan cheese
- Salt and pepper, to taste

Instructions:

1. **Prepare the Eggplant**: Preheat the oven to 375°F (190°C). Lay the eggplant slices on a baking sheet and bake for 10-12 minutes until soft.
2. **Make the Meat Sauce**: In a skillet, cook ground beef or turkey with onion and garlic until browned. Add marinara sauce and simmer for 5 minutes.
3. **Assemble the Lasagna**: In a baking dish, layer eggplant slices, ricotta cheese, meat sauce, and mozzarella. Repeat layers, finishing with mozzarella cheese on top.
4. **Bake**: Bake for 20-25 minutes until the cheese is bubbly and golden.
5. **Serve**: Let the lasagna cool for a few minutes before serving.

Pork Belly with Roasted Brussels Sprouts

Ingredients:

- 1 lb pork belly, skin on
- 1 lb Brussels sprouts, trimmed and halved
- 2 tablespoons olive oil
- Salt and pepper, to taste
- 1 tablespoon garlic powder
- 1 tablespoon rosemary (optional)

Instructions:

1. **Prepare the Pork Belly**: Preheat the oven to 400°F (200°C). Season the pork belly with salt, pepper, garlic powder, and rosemary. Place the pork belly on a baking sheet.
2. **Roast**: Roast the pork belly for 45-50 minutes, flipping halfway through, until crispy on the outside and tender inside.
3. **Roast the Brussels Sprouts**: Toss the Brussels sprouts with olive oil, salt, and pepper. Add to the baking sheet during the last 20 minutes of roasting, turning occasionally.
4. **Serve**: Slice the pork belly and serve with the roasted Brussels sprouts.

Keto Fish Tacos with Avocado Salsa

Ingredients:

- 1 lb white fish fillets (such as tilapia or cod)
- 1 tablespoon olive oil
- 1 teaspoon cumin
- 1 teaspoon chili powder
- Salt and pepper, to taste
- 1 avocado, diced
- 1/2 cup diced tomatoes
- 1/4 cup red onion, finely chopped
- 1 tablespoon fresh cilantro, chopped
- Juice of 1 lime
- Lettuce leaves (for taco wraps)

Instructions:

1. **Cook the Fish**: Heat olive oil in a skillet over medium-high heat. Season the fish with cumin, chili powder, salt, and pepper. Cook for 3-4 minutes per side until flaky and cooked through.
2. **Make the Avocado Salsa**: In a bowl, combine avocado, tomatoes, onion, cilantro, and lime juice. Mix gently and season with salt and pepper.
3. **Assemble the Tacos**: Place the fish fillets in lettuce leaves and top with avocado salsa.
4. **Serve**: Serve immediately and enjoy!

Chicken Thighs with Garlic Mushroom Sauce

Ingredients:

- 4 bone-in, skin-on chicken thighs
- 2 tablespoons olive oil
- 1/2 cup mushrooms, sliced
- 3 cloves garlic, minced
- 1/2 cup heavy cream
- 1/2 cup chicken broth
- Salt and pepper, to taste

Instructions:

1. **Cook the Chicken**: Heat olive oil in a skillet over medium-high heat. Season the chicken thighs with salt and pepper. Cook for 7-8 minutes per side until golden brown and cooked through.
2. **Make the Sauce**: In the same skillet, add mushrooms and garlic. Sauté for 2-3 minutes. Add heavy cream and chicken broth, then simmer until the sauce thickens.
3. **Serve**: Pour the garlic mushroom sauce over the chicken thighs and serve!

Cheesy Broccoli and Cauliflower Casserole

Ingredients:

- 1 cup cauliflower florets
- 1 cup broccoli florets
- 1 cup shredded cheddar cheese
- 1/4 cup heavy cream
- 1/4 cup cream cheese
- 1/2 teaspoon garlic powder
- Salt and pepper, to taste

Instructions:

1. **Preheat the Oven**: Preheat the oven to 375°F (190°C). Grease a baking dish.
2. **Cook the Vegetables**: Steam cauliflower and broccoli until tender (about 10 minutes).
3. **Make the Cheese Sauce**: In a saucepan, melt cream cheese and heavy cream over medium heat. Add garlic powder, salt, and pepper, then stir in shredded cheese until melted and smooth.
4. **Assemble the Casserole**: Combine steamed vegetables with cheese sauce in the baking dish. Stir to coat evenly and bake for 15-20 minutes until bubbly and golden.

Keto Steak with Herb Butter

Ingredients:

- 2 steaks (your choice of cut)
- 2 tablespoons olive oil
- Salt and pepper, to taste
- 1/4 cup butter, softened
- 1 tablespoon fresh parsley, chopped
- 1 teaspoon garlic powder
- 1 teaspoon fresh thyme (optional)

Instructions:

1. **Cook the Steaks**: Heat olive oil in a skillet over high heat. Season the steaks with salt and pepper. Cook for 4-5 minutes per side for medium-rare, or to your preferred doneness.
2. **Make the Herb Butter**: In a small bowl, mix softened butter with parsley, garlic powder, and thyme.
3. **Serve**: Top each steak with a dollop of herb butter and serve immediately.

Grilled Lamb Chops with Mint Yogurt Sauce

Ingredients:

- 8 lamb chops
- 2 tablespoons olive oil
- Salt and pepper, to taste
- 2 cloves garlic, minced
- 1 tablespoon fresh rosemary, chopped
- 1 cup Greek yogurt
- 2 tablespoons fresh mint, chopped
- 1 tablespoon lemon juice
- 1 teaspoon honey (optional)

Instructions:

1. **Marinate the Lamb Chops**:
   In a bowl, combine olive oil, garlic, rosemary, salt, and pepper. Rub the mixture over the lamb chops and let them marinate for at least 30 minutes.
2. **Grill the Lamb Chops**:
   Preheat the grill to medium-high heat. Grill the lamb chops for about 4-5 minutes per side, or until they reach your desired level of doneness.
3. **Make the Mint Yogurt Sauce**:
   In a small bowl, mix Greek yogurt, mint, lemon juice, salt, and pepper. Add honey for a touch of sweetness if desired.
4. **Serve**:
   Serve the grilled lamb chops with a generous dollop of mint yogurt sauce on the side.

Shrimp and Sausage Skillet

Ingredients:

- 1 lb shrimp, peeled and deveined
- 2 sausages (chicken, pork, or turkey), sliced
- 1 tablespoon olive oil
- 1/2 onion, chopped
- 2 cloves garlic, minced
- 1 bell pepper, chopped
- 1/2 teaspoon paprika
- Salt and pepper, to taste
- 1 tablespoon fresh parsley, chopped

Instructions:

1. **Cook the Sausage:**
   Heat olive oil in a large skillet over medium heat. Add the sausage slices and cook until browned, about 5-6 minutes. Remove from the skillet and set aside.
2. **Cook the Vegetables:**
   In the same skillet, add onion, garlic, and bell pepper. Sauté for 3-4 minutes until softened.
3. **Cook the Shrimp:**
   Add shrimp to the skillet along with paprika, salt, and pepper. Cook for 3-4 minutes on each side until the shrimp is pink and cooked through.
4. **Combine and Serve:**
   Add the sausage back to the skillet and stir to combine. Garnish with fresh parsley and serve immediately.

Keto Stuffed Bell Peppers

Ingredients:

- 4 bell peppers, tops cut off and seeds removed
- 1 lb ground beef or turkey
- 1/2 onion, chopped
- 1/2 cup cauliflower rice (or regular rice if not keto)
- 1/2 cup shredded cheese (cheddar or mozzarella)
- 1 teaspoon cumin
- 1 teaspoon paprika
- Salt and pepper, to taste
- 1/2 cup marinara sauce (sugar-free)

Instructions:

1. **Preheat the Oven**:
   Preheat the oven to 375°F (190°C). Place the bell peppers in a baking dish.
2. **Prepare the Filling**:
   In a skillet, cook the ground beef with onion over medium heat until browned. Add cauliflower rice, cumin, paprika, salt, and pepper. Stir to combine and cook for another 5-7 minutes.
3. **Stuff the Peppers**:
   Fill each bell pepper with the beef mixture and top with marinara sauce and shredded cheese.
4. **Bake**:
   Cover the baking dish with foil and bake for 25-30 minutes. Remove the foil for the last 5 minutes to allow the cheese to melt and brown.
5. **Serve**:
   Serve the stuffed peppers hot, garnished with fresh herbs if desired.

Spinach and Feta Stuffed Chicken Breast

Ingredients:

- 4 boneless, skinless chicken breasts
- 1 cup spinach, chopped
- 1/2 cup feta cheese, crumbled
- 2 cloves garlic, minced
- 2 tablespoons olive oil
- Salt and pepper, to taste
- 1 teaspoon oregano (optional)

Instructions:

1. **Preheat the Oven**:
   Preheat the oven to 375°F (190°C).
2. **Prepare the Filling**:
   In a skillet, sauté garlic and spinach in olive oil until the spinach wilts. Let it cool slightly and then mix in feta cheese.
3. **Stuff the Chicken**:
   Slice a pocket into each chicken breast. Stuff the pockets with the spinach and feta mixture. Secure with toothpicks if necessary.
4. **Cook the Chicken**:
   Season the chicken with salt, pepper, and oregano. Heat olive oil in a skillet over medium-high heat. Sear the chicken breasts for 3-4 minutes per side until golden brown. Transfer the chicken to the oven and bake for 20-25 minutes, or until the internal temperature reaches 165°F (75°C).
5. **Serve**:
   Remove the toothpicks and serve hot.

Eggplant and Ground Beef Moussaka

Ingredients:

- 2 large eggplants, sliced into rounds
- 1 lb ground beef
- 1 onion, chopped
- 2 cloves garlic, minced
- 1/2 cup marinara sauce (sugar-free)
- 1 teaspoon cinnamon
- 1/2 cup heavy cream
- 1/2 cup shredded cheese (optional)
- 1 egg
- Salt and pepper, to taste

Instructions:

1. **Prepare the Eggplant**:
   Preheat the oven to 375°F (190°C). Slice the eggplant and arrange on a baking sheet. Roast for 20 minutes until tender and slightly browned.
2. **Cook the Beef**:
   In a skillet, cook the ground beef with onion and garlic until browned. Add marinara sauce, cinnamon, salt, and pepper. Simmer for 10 minutes.
3. **Make the Custard**:
   In a bowl, whisk together the heavy cream, egg, salt, and pepper.
4. **Assemble the Moussaka**:
   In a baking dish, layer roasted eggplant slices, followed by the beef mixture, then repeat. Pour the custard over the top and sprinkle with cheese.
5. **Bake**:
   Bake for 25-30 minutes until the top is golden and bubbly. Let cool slightly before serving.

Lemon Herb Grilled Chicken with Zucchini

Ingredients:

- 4 boneless, skinless chicken breasts
- 2 zucchinis, sliced into rounds
- 2 tablespoons olive oil
- 1 tablespoon lemon zest
- 1 tablespoon fresh thyme, chopped
- 2 cloves garlic, minced
- Salt and pepper, to taste

Instructions:

1. **Marinate the Chicken**:
   In a bowl, combine olive oil, lemon zest, thyme, garlic, salt, and pepper. Marinate the chicken for at least 30 minutes.
2. **Grill the Chicken**:
   Preheat the grill to medium-high heat. Grill the chicken for 6-7 minutes per side, until fully cooked.
3. **Grill the Zucchini**:
   Toss the zucchini slices in olive oil, salt, and pepper, then grill for 2-3 minutes per side until tender and slightly charred.
4. **Serve**:
   Serve the grilled chicken with the zucchini on the side.

Keto Chili with Ground Beef

Ingredients:

- 1 lb ground beef
- 1/2 onion, chopped
- 2 cloves garlic, minced
- 1 can diced tomatoes (no sugar added)
- 1/2 cup beef broth
- 1 tablespoon chili powder
- 1 teaspoon cumin
- 1/2 teaspoon paprika
- Salt and pepper, to taste
- 1/2 cup shredded cheese (optional)
- Sour cream (optional)

Instructions:

1. **Cook the Beef**:
   In a large pot, cook the ground beef with onion and garlic over medium heat until browned.
2. **Simmer the Chili**:
   Add diced tomatoes, beef broth, chili powder, cumin, paprika, salt, and pepper. Simmer for 20-30 minutes, stirring occasionally.
3. **Serve**:
   Top with shredded cheese and sour cream, if desired. Serve hot.

Pork Chops with Avocado Cream Sauce

Ingredients:

- 4 boneless pork chops
- 2 tablespoons olive oil
- Salt and pepper, to taste
- 1 ripe avocado, peeled and pitted
- 1/4 cup sour cream
- 1 tablespoon lime juice
- 1 tablespoon cilantro, chopped

Instructions:

1. **Cook the Pork Chops**:
   Heat olive oil in a skillet over medium-high heat. Season the pork chops with salt and pepper and cook for 5-6 minutes per side until cooked through.
2. **Make the Avocado Sauce**:
   In a blender or food processor, combine avocado, sour cream, lime juice, cilantro, salt, and pepper. Blend until smooth.
3. **Serve**:
   Serve the pork chops with a generous drizzle of avocado cream sauce.

Baked Chicken with Parmesan Crust

Ingredients:

- 4 boneless, skinless chicken breasts
- 1/2 cup grated Parmesan cheese
- 1/2 cup almond flour
- 2 eggs, beaten
- 1 teaspoon garlic powder
- 1 teaspoon dried oregano
- Salt and pepper, to taste

Instructions:

1. **Preheat the Oven**:
   Preheat the oven to 400°F (200°C).
2. **Prepare the Coating**:
   In a shallow bowl, combine Parmesan cheese, almond flour, garlic powder, oregano, salt, and pepper. Dip each chicken breast into the egg, then coat in the Parmesan mixture.
3. **Bake**:
   Place the chicken on a baking sheet and bake for 20-25 minutes, or until the chicken reaches an internal temperature of 165°F (75°C).
4. **Serve**:
   Serve the Parmesan-crusted chicken hot, garnished with fresh herbs if desired.

Keto Meatballs in Tomato Sauce

Ingredients:

- 1 lb ground beef or ground turkey
- 1/4 cup almond flour
- 1/4 cup grated Parmesan cheese
- 1 egg
- 2 cloves garlic, minced
- 1 teaspoon dried oregano
- 1 teaspoon dried basil
- Salt and pepper, to taste
- 2 cups sugar-free marinara sauce
- 1 tablespoon olive oil

Instructions:

1. **Make the Meatballs**:
   In a large bowl, combine ground beef, almond flour, Parmesan, egg, garlic, oregano, basil, salt, and pepper. Mix until well combined. Roll the mixture into 1-inch meatballs.
2. **Cook the Meatballs**:
   Heat olive oil in a large skillet over medium heat. Add the meatballs and cook for about 6-8 minutes, turning occasionally until browned on all sides.
3. **Simmer in Sauce**:
   Pour the marinara sauce over the meatballs and let them simmer for another 10-15 minutes until cooked through.
4. **Serve**:
   Serve the meatballs in the tomato sauce with a sprinkle of Parmesan on top.

Crispy Parmesan Crusted Salmon

Ingredients:

- 4 salmon fillets, skin on
- 1/2 cup grated Parmesan cheese
- 1/4 cup almond flour
- 1 tablespoon garlic powder
- 1 tablespoon dried parsley
- Salt and pepper, to taste
- 2 tablespoons olive oil
- 1 tablespoon lemon juice (optional)

Instructions:

1. **Prepare the Coating**:
   In a shallow bowl, mix together Parmesan cheese, almond flour, garlic powder, parsley, salt, and pepper.
2. **Coat the Salmon**:
   Pat the salmon fillets dry and coat the flesh side with the Parmesan mixture.
3. **Cook the Salmon**:
   Heat olive oil in a skillet over medium-high heat. Add the salmon fillets, skin-side down, and cook for about 4-5 minutes. Flip and cook for another 3-4 minutes, until golden and crispy.
4. **Serve**:
   Serve the salmon with a squeeze of lemon juice and garnish with fresh herbs if desired.

Keto BBQ Ribs

Ingredients:

- 2 racks of baby back ribs
- 1/4 cup olive oil
- Salt and pepper, to taste
- 1/2 cup sugar-free BBQ sauce
- 1 teaspoon garlic powder
- 1 teaspoon smoked paprika
- 1 teaspoon onion powder

Instructions:

1. **Prepare the Ribs**:
   Preheat the oven to 300°F (150°C). Rub the ribs with olive oil, garlic powder, smoked paprika, onion powder, salt, and pepper.
2. **Bake the Ribs**:
   Place the ribs on a baking sheet lined with foil and bake for 2.5 to 3 hours until tender.
3. **Grill and Coat with Sauce**:
   Brush the ribs with sugar-free BBQ sauce and grill for 5-10 minutes on medium heat, basting with more sauce as they cook.
4. **Serve**:
   Cut the ribs between the bones and serve with extra BBQ sauce on the side.

Zucchini and Tomato Gratin

Ingredients:

- 2 zucchinis, sliced thinly
- 2 tomatoes, sliced thinly
- 1/2 cup heavy cream
- 1/2 cup grated Parmesan cheese
- 1/2 cup shredded mozzarella cheese
- 1 tablespoon olive oil
- 1 clove garlic, minced
- Salt and pepper, to taste
- Fresh basil, chopped (optional)

Instructions:

1. **Prepare the Vegetables**:
   Preheat the oven to 375°F (190°C). Layer the zucchini and tomato slices alternately in a baking dish.
2. **Make the Sauce**:
   In a small saucepan, heat olive oil and sauté garlic for 1 minute. Add the heavy cream and simmer for 2-3 minutes. Stir in Parmesan and mozzarella, then season with salt and pepper.
3. **Assemble the Gratin**:
   Pour the cream mixture over the vegetables, then top with extra Parmesan if desired.
4. **Bake**:
   Bake for 25-30 minutes until bubbly and golden on top. Garnish with fresh basil if desired.

Keto Beef Tacos in Lettuce Wraps

Ingredients:

- 1 lb ground beef
- 1 tablespoon olive oil
- 1 small onion, chopped
- 2 cloves garlic, minced
- 1 tablespoon chili powder
- 1 teaspoon cumin
- 1 teaspoon paprika
- Salt and pepper, to taste
- 8 large lettuce leaves (such as romaine or butter lettuce)
- Toppings: sour cream, shredded cheese, diced tomatoes, avocado, cilantro

Instructions:

1. **Cook the Beef**:
   Heat olive oil in a skillet over medium heat. Add onion and garlic, and cook until softened. Add the ground beef, breaking it apart with a spatula. Stir in chili powder, cumin, paprika, salt, and pepper. Cook until browned, about 7-8 minutes.
2. **Assemble the Tacos**:
   Spoon the beef mixture into the center of each lettuce leaf. Top with your favorite taco toppings like sour cream, shredded cheese, diced tomatoes, avocado, and cilantro.
3. **Serve**:
   Serve the tacos immediately and enjoy!

Salmon and Avocado Salad

Ingredients:

- 2 salmon fillets
- 1 tablespoon olive oil
- Salt and pepper, to taste
- 1 ripe avocado, diced
- 4 cups mixed greens (such as arugula, spinach, and lettuce)
- 1/4 cup red onion, thinly sliced
- 1 tablespoon lemon juice
- 2 tablespoons olive oil (for dressing)
- 1 tablespoon Dijon mustard (optional)

Instructions:

1. **Cook the Salmon**:
   Heat olive oil in a skillet over medium-high heat. Season the salmon fillets with salt and pepper and cook for about 4-5 minutes on each side until fully cooked.
2. **Make the Salad**:
   In a large bowl, combine mixed greens, avocado, and red onion.
3. **Prepare the Dressing**:
   Whisk together lemon juice, olive oil, Dijon mustard, salt, and pepper.
4. **Assemble the Salad**:
   Flake the cooked salmon into pieces and add it to the salad. Drizzle the dressing over the salad and toss to combine.

Keto Chicken and Vegetable Stir-Fry

Ingredients:

- 2 chicken breasts, thinly sliced
- 1 tablespoon olive oil
- 1/2 cup bell peppers, sliced
- 1/2 cup zucchini, sliced
- 1/2 cup broccoli florets
- 2 cloves garlic, minced
- 2 tablespoons soy sauce (or coconut aminos for keto)
- 1 tablespoon sesame oil
- Salt and pepper, to taste
- 1 tablespoon sesame seeds (optional)

Instructions:

1. **Cook the Chicken:**
   Heat olive oil in a skillet or wok over medium-high heat. Add the chicken slices and cook until browned and cooked through, about 5-7 minutes. Remove from the pan and set aside.
2. **Stir-Fry the Vegetables:**
   In the same skillet, add more olive oil if needed. Sauté garlic, bell peppers, zucchini, and broccoli for 3-4 minutes until tender but still crisp.
3. **Combine and Serve:**
   Return the chicken to the pan and stir in soy sauce and sesame oil. Cook for another 1-2 minutes to heat through. Serve with a sprinkle of sesame seeds.

Garlic Butter Steak Bites

Ingredients:

- 1 lb sirloin or ribeye steak, cut into bite-sized cubes
- 2 tablespoons olive oil
- 4 tablespoons butter
- 3 cloves garlic, minced
- 1 teaspoon fresh thyme (optional)
- Salt and pepper, to taste
- Fresh parsley, chopped (optional)

Instructions:

1. **Cook the Steak**:
   Heat olive oil in a large skillet over high heat. Season the steak cubes with salt and pepper, then sear them in batches for 2-3 minutes until browned on all sides. Remove from the skillet and set aside.
2. **Make the Garlic Butter**:
   In the same skillet, melt the butter. Add garlic and thyme, cooking for 1 minute until fragrant.
3. **Combine and Serve**:
   Return the steak bites to the skillet and toss in the garlic butter. Cook for another 2-3 minutes. Garnish with parsley and serve.

Cauliflower Mac and Cheese

Ingredients:

- 1 medium head of cauliflower, cut into florets
- 2 tablespoons butter
- 1/2 cup heavy cream
- 1 cup shredded cheddar cheese
- 1/2 cup shredded mozzarella cheese
- Salt and pepper, to taste
- 1/4 teaspoon garlic powder (optional)
- 1/4 teaspoon paprika (optional)

Instructions:

1. **Cook the Cauliflower**:
   Steam the cauliflower florets until tender, about 10-12 minutes.
2. **Make the Cheese Sauce**:
   In a saucepan, melt butter over medium heat. Add heavy cream, cheddar cheese, mozzarella, salt, pepper, garlic powder, and paprika. Stir until the cheese is melted and smooth.
3. **Combine**:
   Pour the cheese sauce over the steamed cauliflower and toss to coat.
4. **Serve**:
   Serve warm and enjoy this low-carb mac and cheese alternative!

Keto Beef Wellington

Ingredients:

- 1 lb beef tenderloin
- 2 tablespoons olive oil
- Salt and pepper, to taste
- 8 oz mushrooms, finely chopped
- 1/4 cup heavy cream
- 1/4 cup Parmesan cheese
- 1 egg (for egg wash)
- 1 sheet keto puff pastry (store-bought or homemade)

Instructions:

1. **Prepare the Beef**:
   Preheat the oven to 400°F (200°C). Season the beef tenderloin with salt and pepper. Heat olive oil in a skillet over high heat and sear the beef on all sides until browned (about 2-3 minutes). Let the beef cool completely.
2. **Make the Mushroom Filling**:
   In the same skillet, sauté the chopped mushrooms until all the moisture evaporates. Add heavy cream and Parmesan cheese, cooking until the mixture thickens and becomes paste-like. Let cool.
3. **Assemble the Wellington**:
   Roll out the keto puff pastry on a parchment paper. Spread the mushroom mixture over the beef, then wrap the beef with the pastry. Brush the pastry with egg wash.
4. **Bake**:
   Place the wrapped beef on a baking sheet and bake for 25-30 minutes, until the pastry is golden brown. Let rest before slicing.

Keto Shrimp Scampi

Ingredients:

- 1 lb large shrimp, peeled and deveined
- 3 tablespoons butter
- 4 cloves garlic, minced
- 1/4 teaspoon red pepper flakes (optional)
- 1/2 cup white wine (or chicken broth)
- 2 tablespoons fresh lemon juice
- 2 tablespoons fresh parsley, chopped
- Zucchini noodles or shirataki noodles (for serving)

Instructions:

1. **Cook the Shrimp:**
   In a large skillet, melt butter over medium heat. Add the garlic and red pepper flakes (if using) and sauté for 1 minute until fragrant.
2. **Make the Sauce:**
   Add the shrimp to the skillet and cook for 2-3 minutes per side until pink. Pour in the white wine and lemon juice, stirring to combine. Let the sauce reduce for a few minutes.
3. **Serve:**
   Serve the shrimp scampi over zucchini noodles or shirataki noodles. Garnish with parsley and extra lemon juice.

Crab Cakes with Lemon Aioli

Ingredients:

- 1 lb lump crab meat
- 1/4 cup almond flour
- 1/4 cup mayonnaise
- 1 egg
- 2 tablespoons Dijon mustard
- 1 tablespoon lemon juice
- 1 tablespoon fresh parsley, chopped
- Salt and pepper, to taste
- Olive oil for frying

For the Lemon Aioli:

- 1/2 cup mayonnaise
- 1 tablespoon lemon juice
- 1 clove garlic, minced
- Salt and pepper, to taste

Instructions:

1. **Make the Crab Cakes**:
   In a large bowl, combine crab meat, almond flour, mayonnaise, egg, Dijon mustard, lemon juice, parsley, salt, and pepper. Gently mix together and form into small patties.
2. **Cook the Crab Cakes**:
   Heat olive oil in a skillet over medium heat. Cook the crab cakes for 3-4 minutes per side, until golden brown and crispy.
3. **Make the Aioli**:
   In a small bowl, mix together mayonnaise, lemon juice, garlic, salt, and pepper.
4. **Serve**:
   Serve the crab cakes with lemon aioli on the side.

Keto Broccoli Cheese Soup

Ingredients:

- 4 cups broccoli florets
- 1/2 cup chopped onion
- 3 cloves garlic, minced
- 4 cups chicken broth
- 1/2 cup heavy cream
- 2 cups shredded cheddar cheese
- 1 teaspoon salt
- 1/2 teaspoon black pepper
- 2 tablespoons olive oil

Instructions:

1. **Cook the Vegetables**:
   Heat olive oil in a large pot over medium heat. Add the onion and garlic and sauté until softened. Add the broccoli and chicken broth and bring to a boil.
2. **Simmer**:
   Reduce the heat and simmer for 10-15 minutes until the broccoli is tender.
3. **Make the Soup**:
   Use an immersion blender to blend the soup until smooth, or leave some chunks for texture. Stir in the heavy cream and shredded cheddar cheese, continuing to stir until the cheese melts.
4. **Serve**:
   Season with salt and pepper, and serve hot.

Grilled Chicken with Avocado Salsa

Ingredients:

- 4 boneless, skinless chicken breasts
- 2 tablespoons olive oil
- Salt and pepper, to taste
- 1 teaspoon chili powder
- 1 teaspoon cumin

For the Avocado Salsa:

- 2 avocados, diced
- 1 small tomato, diced
- 1/4 cup red onion, finely chopped
- 1 tablespoon lime juice
- 1/4 cup cilantro, chopped
- Salt and pepper, to taste

Instructions:

1. **Grill the Chicken**:
   Preheat the grill to medium-high heat. Rub the chicken breasts with olive oil, salt, pepper, chili powder, and cumin. Grill the chicken for 5-7 minutes per side, or until fully cooked.
2. **Make the Avocado Salsa**:
   In a bowl, combine the diced avocados, tomato, onion, lime juice, cilantro, salt, and pepper.
3. **Serve**:
   Top the grilled chicken with the avocado salsa and serve immediately.

Keto Pork Stir Fry

Ingredients:

- 1 lb pork tenderloin, sliced thinly
- 2 tablespoons olive oil
- 1 bell pepper, sliced
- 1 zucchini, sliced
- 1/2 cup broccoli florets
- 2 tablespoons soy sauce (or coconut aminos for keto)
- 1 tablespoon sesame oil
- 2 cloves garlic, minced
- Salt and pepper, to taste
- 1 tablespoon sesame seeds (optional)

Instructions:

1. **Cook the Pork**:
   Heat olive oil in a skillet over medium-high heat. Add the sliced pork and cook until browned and cooked through, about 5-7 minutes. Remove from the pan and set aside.
2. **Stir-Fry the Vegetables**:
   In the same skillet, add more oil if needed. Add garlic, bell pepper, zucchini, and broccoli. Stir-fry for 4-5 minutes until the vegetables are tender.
3. **Combine and Serve**:
   Return the pork to the skillet and stir in soy sauce and sesame oil. Cook for another 2-3 minutes until heated through. Garnish with sesame seeds.

Creamy Tuscan Chicken

Ingredients:

- 4 boneless, skinless chicken breasts
- 2 tablespoons olive oil
- Salt and pepper, to taste
- 1/2 cup sun-dried tomatoes, chopped
- 1/2 cup heavy cream
- 1/2 cup chicken broth
- 1/2 cup spinach, chopped
- 1/4 cup Parmesan cheese
- 1 teaspoon garlic powder

Instructions:

1. **Cook the Chicken**:
   Heat olive oil in a skillet over medium-high heat. Season the chicken breasts with salt, pepper, and garlic powder. Cook the chicken for 6-7 minutes per side until fully cooked. Remove and set aside.
2. **Make the Sauce**:
   In the same skillet, add the sun-dried tomatoes, heavy cream, chicken broth, and spinach. Simmer for 3-4 minutes until the sauce thickens. Stir in Parmesan cheese.
3. **Serve**:
   Return the chicken to the skillet and coat with the creamy sauce. Serve hot.

Keto Mushroom and Swiss Burger

Ingredients:

- 1 lb ground beef
- Salt and pepper, to taste
- 1 tablespoon olive oil
- 1/2 cup mushrooms, sliced
- 2 slices Swiss cheese
- Lettuce leaves (for wrapping)

Instructions:

1. **Make the Patties**:
   Season the ground beef with salt and pepper and form into burger patties.
2. **Cook the Burgers**:
   Heat olive oil in a skillet over medium-high heat. Cook the burger patties for 5-7 minutes per side, or until desired doneness.
3. **Sauté the Mushrooms**:
   In the same skillet, sauté the sliced mushrooms until tender, about 3 minutes.
4. **Assemble**:
   Top each burger with Swiss cheese and sautéed mushrooms. Serve wrapped in lettuce leaves.

Eggplant Parmesan

Ingredients:

- 2 medium eggplants, sliced into rounds
- 1 cup almond flour
- 1 cup grated Parmesan cheese
- 2 eggs, beaten
- 2 cups sugar-free marinara sauce
- 1 cup shredded mozzarella cheese
- 2 tablespoons olive oil
- Salt and pepper, to taste
- Fresh basil (for garnish)

Instructions:

1. **Prepare the Eggplant**:
   Preheat the oven to 375°F (190°C). Dip the eggplant slices into beaten eggs, then coat in a mixture of almond flour, Parmesan, salt, and pepper.
2. **Bake the Eggplant**:
   Place the breaded eggplant slices on a baking sheet and bake for 20-25 minutes, flipping halfway through.
3. **Assemble the Dish**:
   In a baking dish, layer the eggplant slices with marinara sauce and mozzarella cheese. Repeat the layers, then bake for another 10 minutes until the cheese is bubbly and golden.
4. **Serve**:
   Garnish with fresh basil and serve hot.

Keto Cabbage Stir Fry

Ingredients:

- 4 cups shredded cabbage
- 2 tablespoons olive oil
- 1 onion, sliced
- 2 cloves garlic, minced
- 1 bell pepper, sliced
- 1/2 cup soy sauce (or coconut aminos for keto)
- 1 tablespoon sesame oil
- 1 teaspoon ground ginger
- Salt and pepper, to taste
- 1/4 cup green onions, sliced (for garnish)

Instructions:

1. **Cook the Vegetables**:
   Heat olive oil in a large skillet or wok over medium-high heat. Add the onion, garlic, bell pepper, and cook for 3-4 minutes until softened.
2. **Add the Cabbage**:
   Add the shredded cabbage to the pan and stir-fry for about 5-7 minutes until the cabbage begins to soften but still has a slight crunch.
3. **Season and Serve**:
   Stir in soy sauce, sesame oil, ground ginger, salt, and pepper. Cook for an additional 2-3 minutes. Garnish with sliced green onions and serve.

Keto Stuffed Mushrooms

Ingredients:

- 12 large mushrooms, stems removed
- 4 oz cream cheese, softened
- 1/4 cup grated Parmesan cheese
- 1/4 cup chopped spinach
- 2 cloves garlic, minced
- Salt and pepper, to taste
- 1 tablespoon olive oil
- 1/4 cup shredded mozzarella cheese (optional, for topping)

Instructions:

1. **Prepare the Mushrooms**:
   Preheat the oven to 375°F (190°C). Clean the mushroom caps and remove the stems. Set aside.
2. **Make the Filling**:
   In a bowl, combine the cream cheese, Parmesan, spinach, garlic, salt, and pepper. Mix well until smooth.
3. **Stuff the Mushrooms**:
   Spoon the filling into each mushroom cap. Place the stuffed mushrooms on a baking sheet and drizzle with olive oil.
4. **Bake**:
   Bake for 20-25 minutes until the mushrooms are tender and the filling is golden. If using mozzarella, sprinkle it over the stuffed mushrooms 5 minutes before they're done baking.

Chicken Alfredo with Zucchini Noodles

Ingredients:

- 2 boneless, skinless chicken breasts
- 2 tablespoons olive oil
- Salt and pepper, to taste
- 3 medium zucchini, spiralized into noodles
- 1/2 cup heavy cream
- 1/2 cup grated Parmesan cheese
- 1 clove garlic, minced
- 2 tablespoons butter
- Fresh parsley, chopped (for garnish)

Instructions:

1. **Cook the Chicken**:
   Season the chicken breasts with salt and pepper. Heat olive oil in a skillet over medium-high heat. Cook the chicken for 6-7 minutes per side until golden and cooked through. Slice the chicken thinly.
2. **Prepare the Alfredo Sauce**:
   In the same skillet, melt the butter and sauté the garlic for 1 minute. Add the heavy cream and bring to a simmer. Stir in Parmesan cheese and cook until the sauce thickens.
3. **Cook the Zucchini Noodles**:
   In another pan, sauté the zucchini noodles with a little olive oil for 2-3 minutes until just tender.
4. **Assemble**:
   Toss the zucchini noodles in the Alfredo sauce and top with the sliced chicken. Garnish with fresh parsley and serve.

Keto Chicken Piccata

Ingredients:

- 4 boneless, skinless chicken breasts
- Salt and pepper, to taste
- 1/4 cup almond flour
- 2 tablespoons olive oil
- 2 tablespoons butter
- 1/4 cup lemon juice
- 1/4 cup chicken broth
- 2 tablespoons capers
- Fresh parsley, chopped (for garnish)

Instructions:

1. **Prepare the Chicken**:
   Season the chicken breasts with salt and pepper. Dredge each breast in almond flour, shaking off excess.
2. **Cook the Chicken**:
   Heat olive oil in a skillet over medium-high heat. Cook the chicken breasts for 4-5 minutes per side until golden and cooked through. Remove the chicken and set aside.
3. **Make the Piccata Sauce**:
   In the same skillet, melt butter and add lemon juice, chicken broth, and capers. Simmer for 3-4 minutes until the sauce slightly thickens.
4. **Serve**:
   Return the chicken to the skillet and spoon the sauce over it. Garnish with fresh parsley and serve.

Beef and Broccoli Stir Fry

Ingredients:

- 1 lb beef sirloin or flank steak, thinly sliced
- 2 tablespoons olive oil
- 1 onion, sliced
- 2 cups broccoli florets
- 2 tablespoons soy sauce (or coconut aminos for keto)
- 1 tablespoon oyster sauce
- 1 teaspoon garlic powder
- Salt and pepper, to taste
- 1 tablespoon sesame seeds (optional)

Instructions:

1. **Cook the Beef**:
   Heat 1 tablespoon of olive oil in a skillet over medium-high heat. Add the beef and cook for 3-4 minutes until browned. Remove and set aside.
2. **Stir-Fry the Vegetables**:
   In the same skillet, add the remaining olive oil. Add onion and broccoli, and stir-fry for 5-7 minutes until tender.
3. **Combine**:
   Return the beef to the skillet. Stir in soy sauce, oyster sauce, garlic powder, salt, and pepper. Cook for 2 more minutes, stirring to coat the beef and vegetables in the sauce.
4. **Serve**:
   Garnish with sesame seeds, and serve immediately.

Crispy Skin Duck Breast with Cauliflower Puree

Ingredients:

- 2 duck breasts
- Salt and pepper, to taste
- 1 tablespoon olive oil
- 2 cups cauliflower florets
- 1/4 cup heavy cream
- 2 tablespoons butter
- Garlic powder, to taste

Instructions:

1. **Prepare the Duck Breasts:**
   Score the skin of the duck breasts with a knife and season with salt and pepper. Heat olive oil in a pan over medium-high heat. Place the duck breasts skin-side down and cook for 6-8 minutes until the skin is crispy. Flip and cook for another 4-5 minutes until the duck is cooked to your liking.
2. **Make the Cauliflower Puree:**
   Steam the cauliflower florets until tender, about 10 minutes. Transfer to a blender and add heavy cream, butter, salt, pepper, and garlic powder. Blend until smooth.
3. **Serve:**
   Plate the crispy duck breasts over the cauliflower puree and serve immediately.

Keto Shrimp and Avocado Salad

Ingredients:

- 1 lb shrimp, peeled and deveined
- 1 tablespoon olive oil
- Salt and pepper, to taste
- 2 avocados, diced
- 2 cups mixed greens
- 1 cucumber, sliced
- 1/4 cup red onion, thinly sliced
- 1/4 cup fresh cilantro, chopped
- 1 tablespoon lime juice

Instructions:

1. **Cook the Shrimp**:
   Heat olive oil in a skillet over medium-high heat. Season the shrimp with salt and pepper, then cook for 2-3 minutes per side until pink and cooked through.
2. **Prepare the Salad**:
   In a large bowl, combine the mixed greens, diced avocados, cucumber, red onion, and cilantro. Drizzle with lime juice.
3. **Serve**:
   Top the salad with the cooked shrimp and serve immediately.

Keto Cheeseburger Salad

Ingredients:

- 1 lb ground beef
- Salt and pepper, to taste
- 4 cups mixed greens
- 1/2 cup shredded cheddar cheese
- 1/4 cup pickles, sliced
- 1/4 cup red onion, sliced
- 1/4 cup sugar-free ketchup
- 1 tablespoon mustard

Instructions:

1. **Cook the Ground Beef**:
   Season the ground beef with salt and pepper. Cook in a skillet over medium heat until browned and fully cooked.
2. **Assemble the Salad**:
   In a large bowl, combine the mixed greens, cheddar cheese, pickles, and red onion. Toss with the ketchup and mustard.
3. **Serve**:
   Top the salad with the cooked ground beef and serve immediately.

Grilled Pork Tenderloin with Garlic Butter

Ingredients:

- 1 lb pork tenderloin
- 2 tablespoons olive oil
- Salt and pepper, to taste
- 1/4 cup butter
- 3 cloves garlic, minced
- 1 tablespoon fresh parsley, chopped

Instructions:

1. **Grill the Pork**:
   Preheat the grill to medium-high heat. Season the pork tenderloin with olive oil, salt, and pepper. Grill for 20-25 minutes, turning occasionally, until the pork reaches an internal temperature of 145°F (63°C).
2. **Make the Garlic Butter**:
   Melt butter in a skillet over medium heat. Add garlic and sauté for 1-2 minutes until fragrant.
3. **Serve**:
   Drizzle the garlic butter over the grilled pork tenderloin and garnish with fresh parsley.

Keto Shrimp and Spinach Casserole

Ingredients:

- 1 lb shrimp, peeled and deveined
- 2 cups spinach, chopped
- 1 cup heavy cream
- 1/2 cup grated Parmesan cheese
- 1 tablespoon butter
- 1 clove garlic, minced
- Salt and pepper, to taste

Instructions:

1. **Cook the Shrimp**:
   In a skillet, melt butter over medium heat. Add the shrimp and cook for 2-3 minutes per side until pink and cooked through. Remove and set aside.
2. **Make the Casserole**:
   In the same skillet, sauté garlic for 1 minute. Add spinach and cook until wilted. Pour in heavy cream, Parmesan, salt, and pepper. Simmer for 2-3 minutes until the sauce thickens.
3. **Assemble**:
   Add the shrimp back to the skillet and stir to combine. Transfer the mixture to a casserole dish and bake at 375°F (190°C) for 10 minutes.
4. **Serve**:
   Serve hot from the casserole dish.

www.ingramcontent.com/pod-product-compliance
Lightning Source LLC
LaVergne TN
LVHW081327060526
838201LV00055B/2506